Tiny Tinkles Little Musicians Series

Little Performers

Patterns on the Black Keys

Created by **Debra Krol** Pictures by **Corinne Orazietti & Melanie Hawkins**

This book is dedicated to
all the little people for inspiring me,
and all the BIG people for believing in me.

Copyright © 2021 Tiny Tinkles Publishing Company

All Rights Reserved.

No parts of this publication or the characters in it, may be reproduced or distributed in any form or by any means without written permission from the publisher.

To request permission, or for school visits and book readings, please visit www.tinytinkles.com

ISBN (Paperback Perfect Bound): 978-1-7777050-7-7

First Edition 2021

TIPS TO HELP YOU TEACH USING THIS BOOK

Welcome to the Tiny Tinkles Little Musicians Series!

In this book your little musician will learn the basics of reading music notation and gain a full understanding of the groups of black notes on the piano.

ACTIVITY CARDS are located in the middle of this book. Remove the page, laminate the full sheet, then cut into individual cards for hours of piano fun. If laminating isn't possible, cut the cards out and glue them onto a sheet of cardstock.

The ACTIVITY CARDS can be placed between the keys of the piano and the fallboard. This is extremely helpful for little musicians because their bodies are so small they struggle with their peripheral vision when they look up so HIGH to see their books on the music stand of the piano.

When playing the patterns and songs in this book, try to keep a very steady beat, like the tik-tock of a clock.

As you progress in the book, some notes will be longer than others. You will see the word HOLD, HOLD DOT or GREAT BIG HOLD ~ say these words OUT LOUD so your little musician can FEEL the beat and rythm of the music.

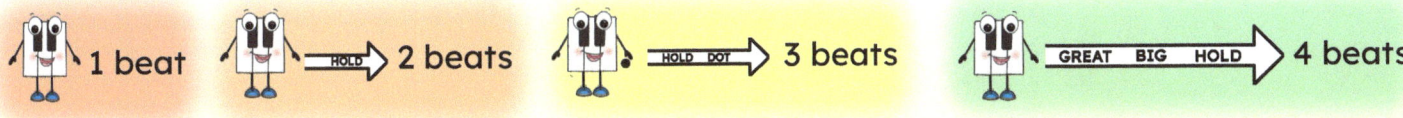

For videos, worksheets, teaching tips and more... please visit: **www.tinytinkles.com**

 It's another musical day in **Tiny Tinkles Town.**

Two new friends have just moved to town. Meet...

TWOOZIE and **THREEZIE.**

Twoozie has **TWO** black notes.
Threezie has **THREE** black notes.
Let's count them! 1, 2... 1, 2, 3.

Twoozie and **Threezie** are excited to learn music.

But most of all... they can't wait to play with you!

Draw a picture of... YOU.

Twoozie and **Threezie** LOVE playing the piano keys!

First... they play down LOW.

Then... they play up HIGH.

Can you find **Twoozie** and **Threezie**'s notes?

Missy Mouse and Parker Penguin LOVE to play on

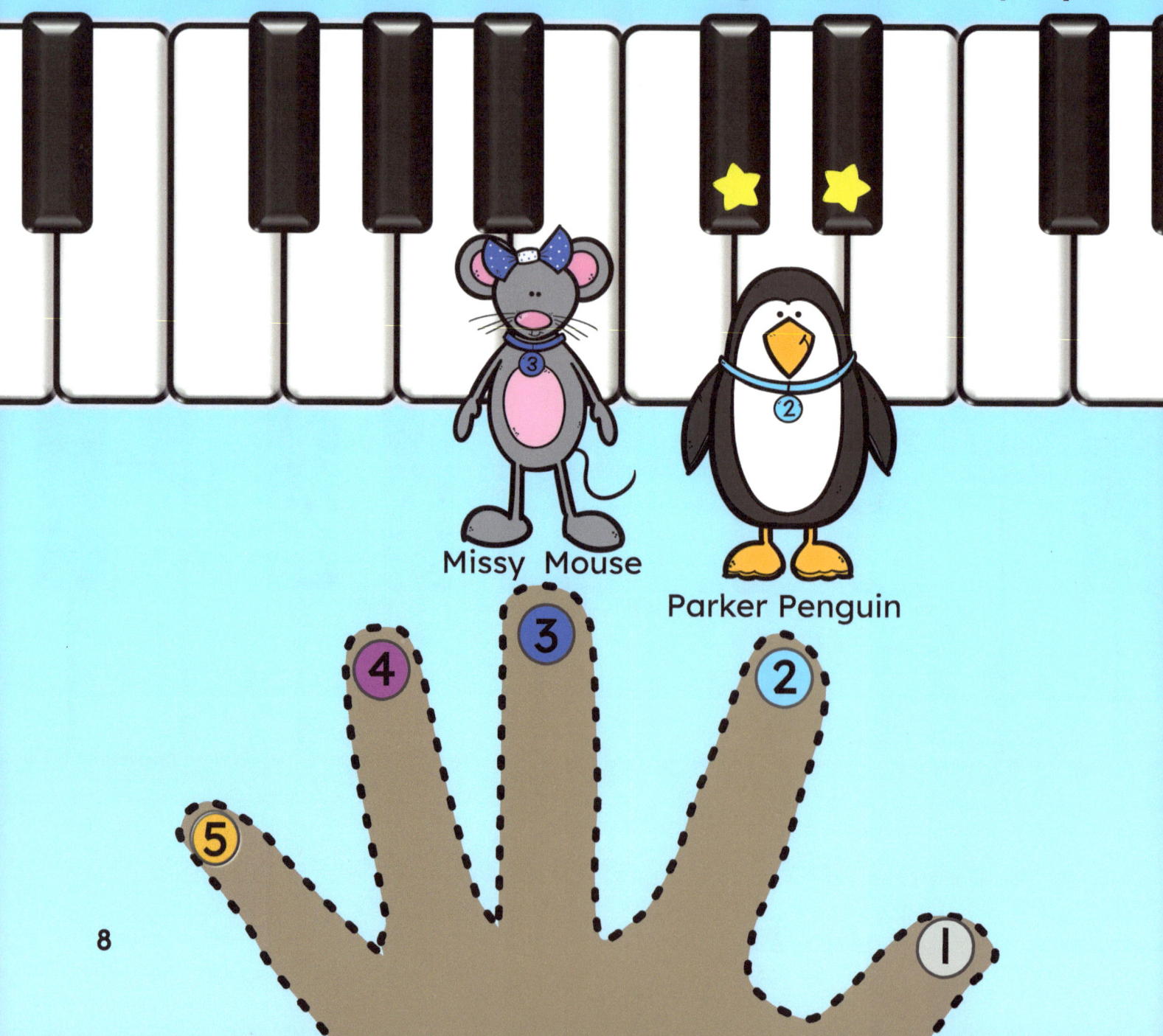

Bobby Bass is practicing **Twoozies** LOW sounds.

Can you help them play together? Play the pattern on **Twoozie's** LOW notes with your LEFT Hand.

Tina Treble practices **Twoozies** HIGH sounds.

Can you help them play together? Follow the pattern on **Twoozie's** HIGH notes with your RIGHT Hand.

Tina Treble is excited to play the piano with **Threezie.**

So now, Parker Penguin, Missy Mouse, Rosie Rabbit, and Bobby Bass play on **Threezies** black keys.

Suddenly, Bobby Bass realizes something he's never noticed before! The black keys on the piano make a **pattern** of two and three.

Bobby Bass has an AMAZING IDEA! He plays all the **TWOOZIES** and **THREEZIES** he can see.

Tina Treble is AMAZED! Bobby Bass's song with **Twoozie** and **Threezie** was beautiful, now it is her turn to play.

Tina Treble listens carefully… and she hears **Twoozie** and **Threezie** singing higher each time she plays.

Making new friends in Tiny Tinkles Town is so much fun.

Tina Treble, Bobby Bass, Parker Penguin, Missy Mouse, Rosie Rabbit, **Twoozie** and **Threezie** play together all day long and make up fun songs together.

Now... it's time for us to learn their songs!

Let's practice some PATTERNS!

Practice Tips! Try playing the patterns in different ways. Start one hand at a time, then try with the other hand. As it gets easier to play hands seperately, try to play hands together dividing the notes between the two hands (LH plays low notes, RH plays high notes). Play them HIGH, LOW, forte LOUD, piano SOFT, lento SLOW and allegro FAST. You can also make a long TRAIN with all the cards.

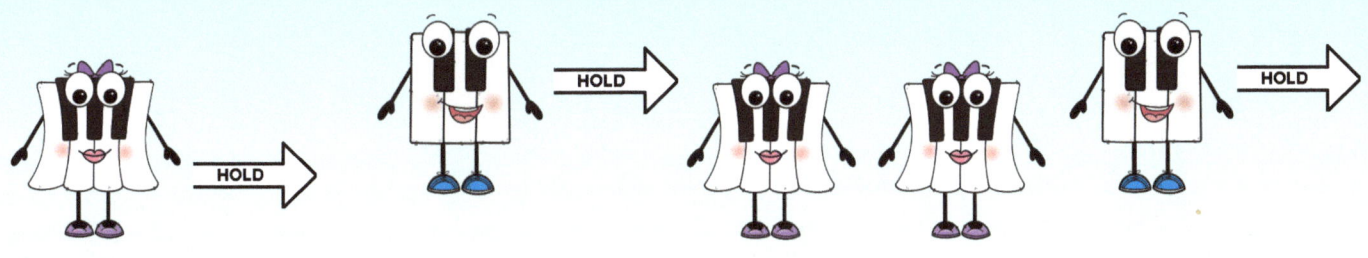
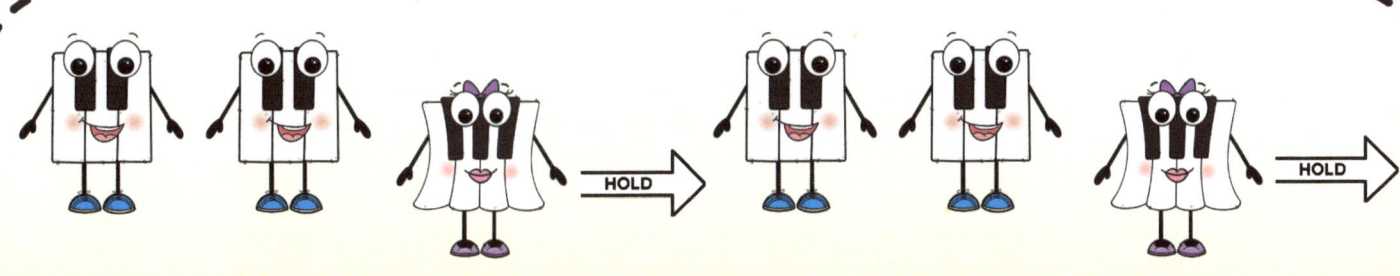

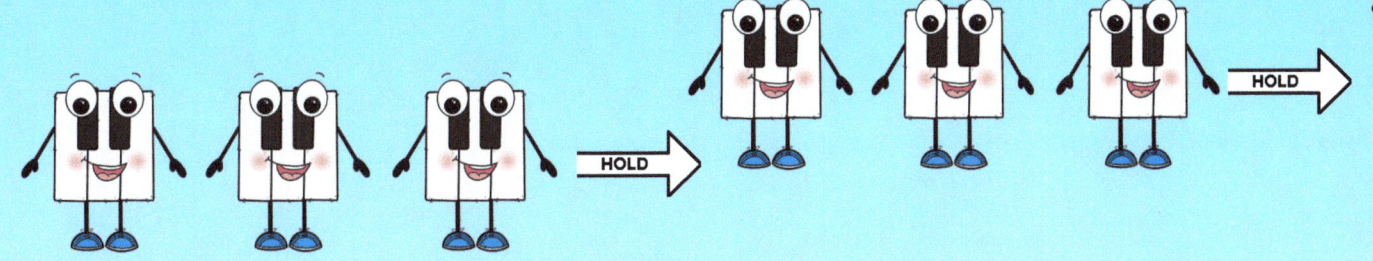
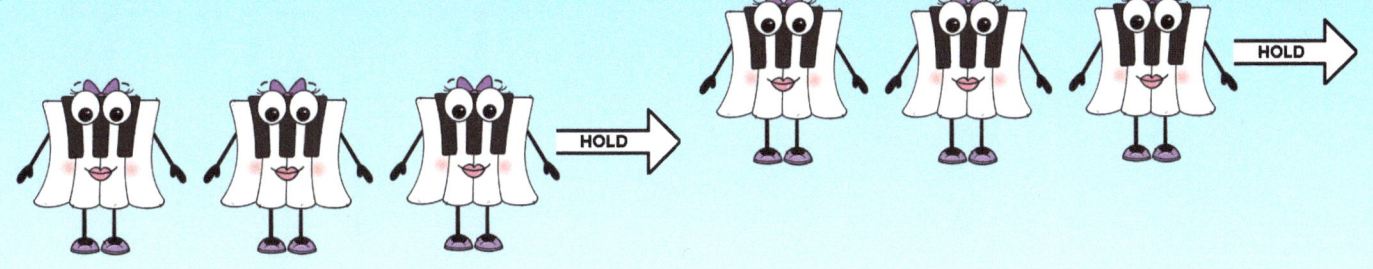

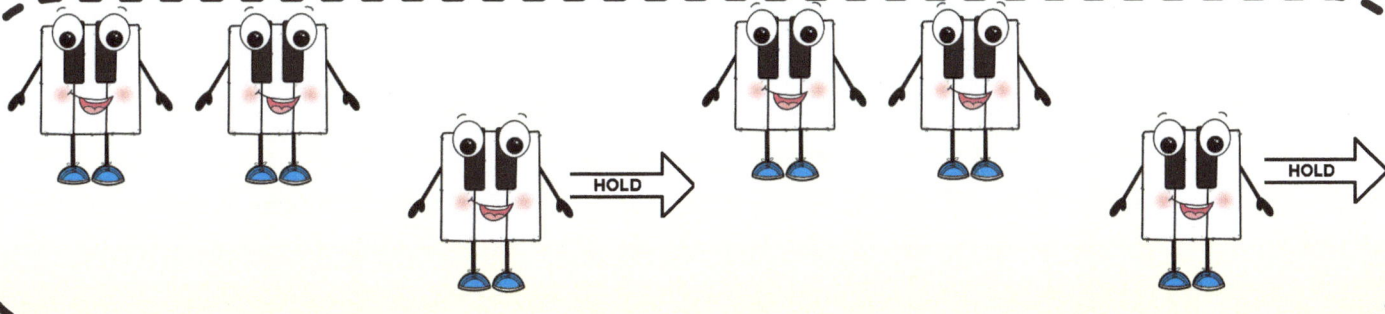

Tiny Tinkles Little Musician Practice Piano

Use these Practice Pianos to practice the patterns and songs in this book off bench. Perfect for group lessons!

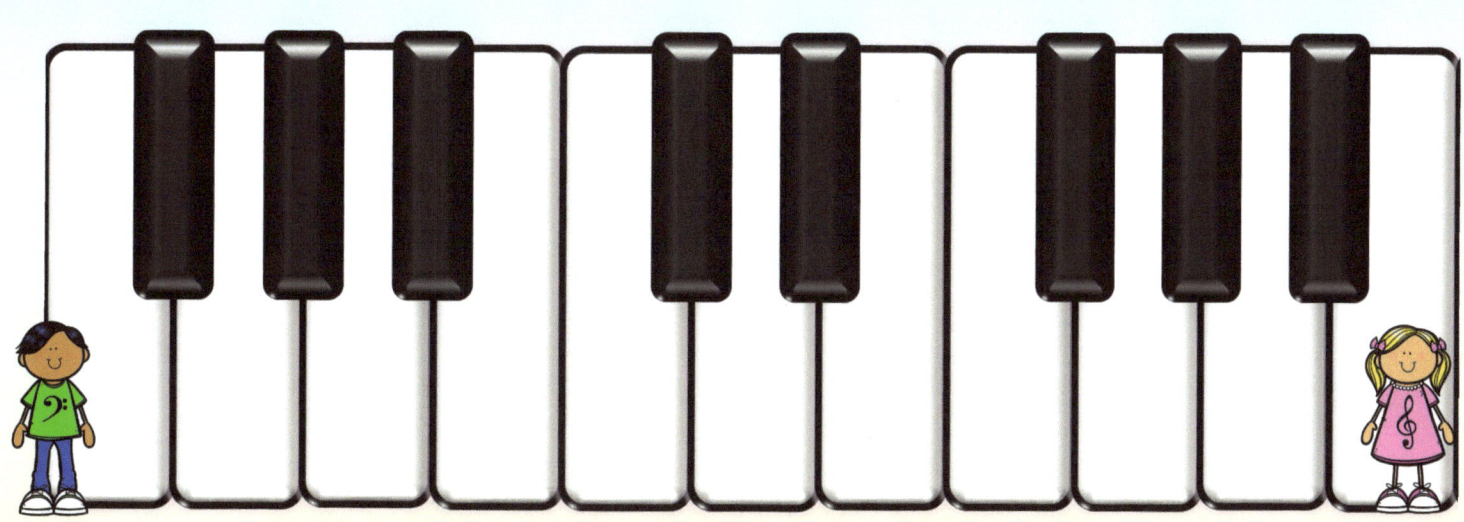

Tiny Tinkles Little Musician Practice Piano

Now... lets practice reading music with Grammy Treble Clef and Grampy Bass Clef!

PLAY 𝄢 Grampy Bass Clef with your LEFT HAND

PLAY 𝄞 Grammy Treble Clef with your RIGHT HAND

Tina Plays Groups of 2

Play **Twoozie**'s black notes with Fingers 2 and 3.
Can you find Parker Penguin and Missy Mouse on your right hand?

count 1 2 3

low

low

low

Color a star each time you practice this song.

Tips for Practicing
Count slowly to three before you begin.
Tap the notes on your lap and sing LOW and HIGH.
Play and sing LOW and HIGH while you play piano.

high   high   high

Bobby Plays Groups of 2

Play **Twoozie**'s black notes with Fingers 3 and 2.
Can you find Missy Mouse and Parker Penguin on your left hand?

Color a star each time you practice this song.

Tips for Practicing
Count slowly to four before you begin.
Tap the notes on your lap and sing LOW and HIGH.
Play and sing LOW and HIGH while you play piano.

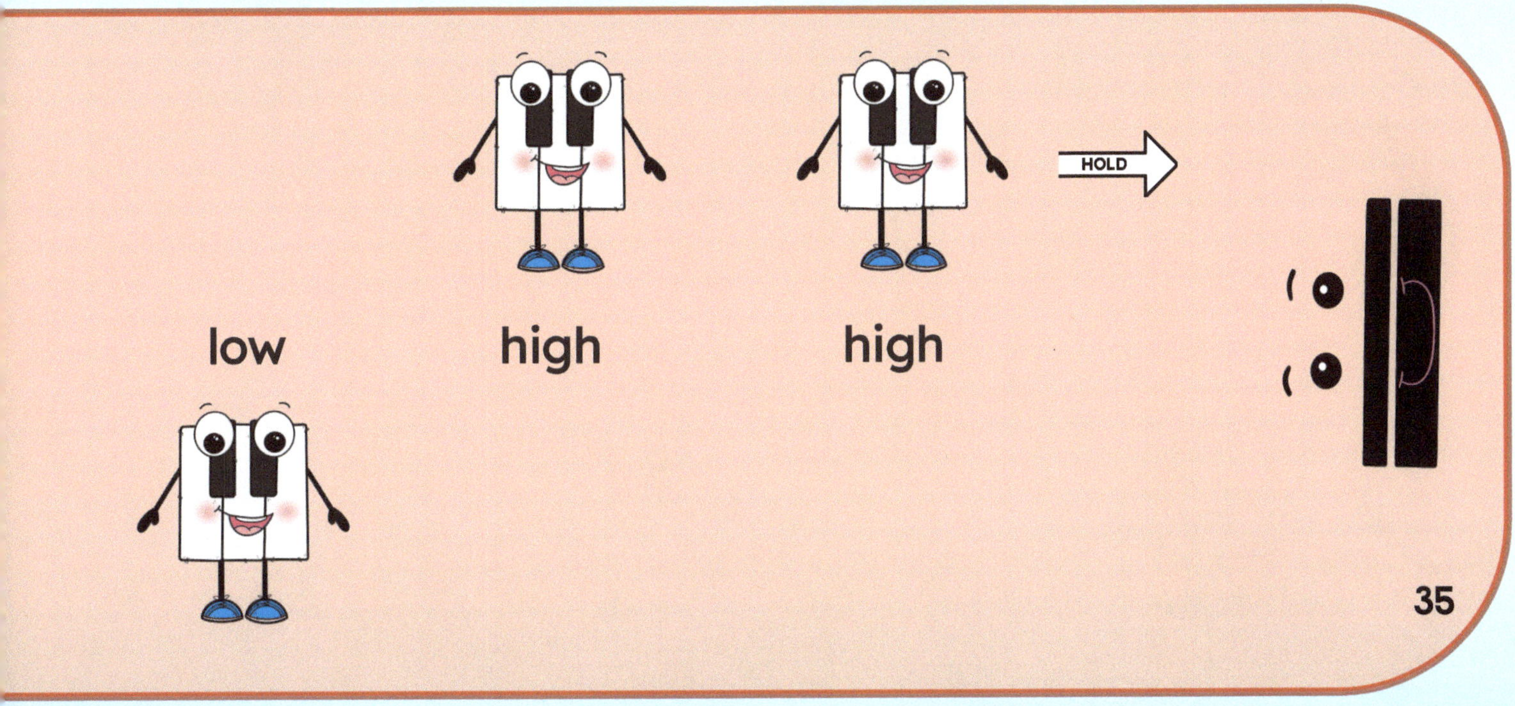

low   high   high   HOLD

Let's Play Both Hands

Play **Twoozie**'s black notes with Fingers 2 and 3.
Find Parker Penguin and Missy Mouse on your hands.

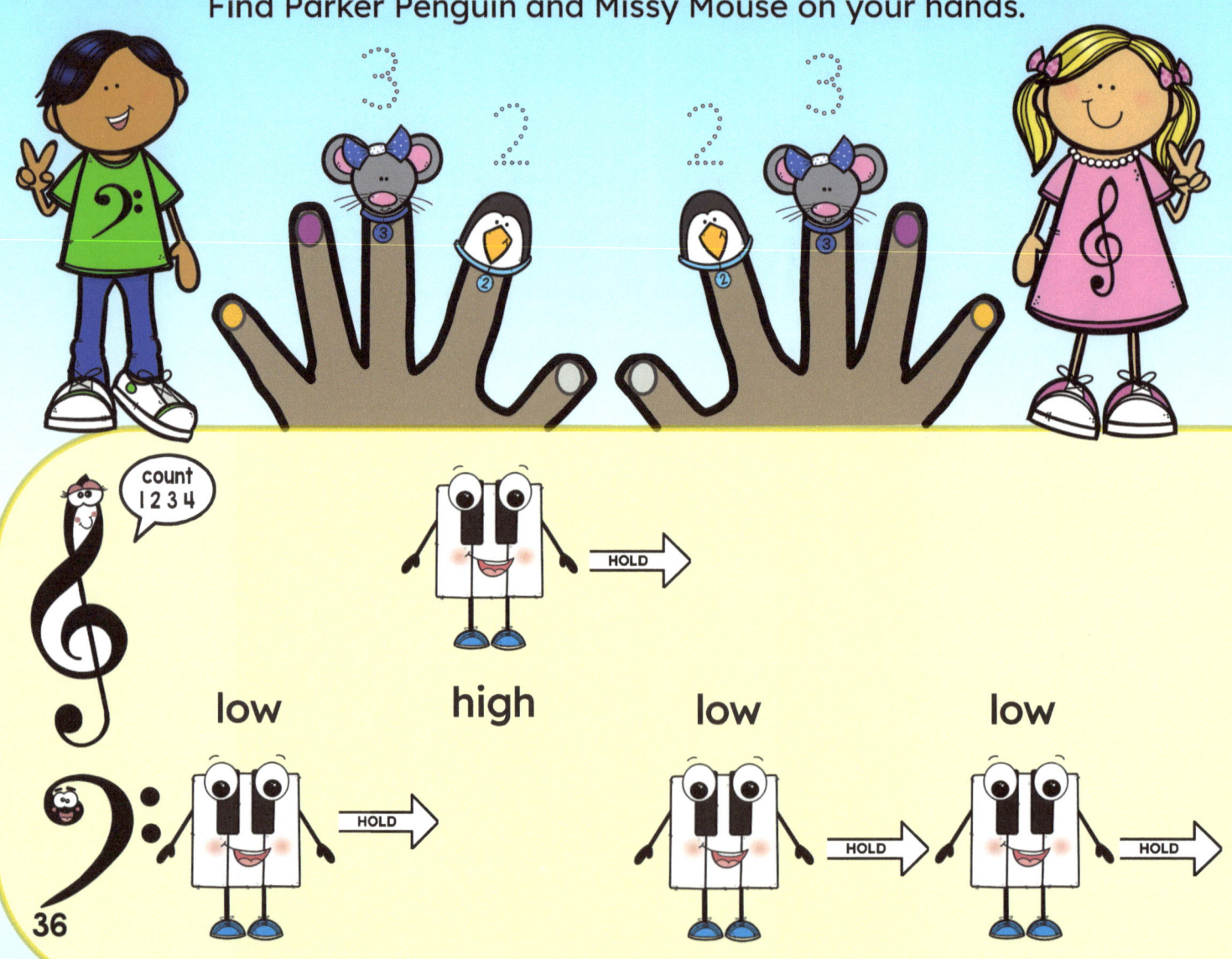

Color a star each time you practice this song.

Tips for Practicing
Count slowly to four before you begin.
the notes on your lap and sing LOW and HIGH.
Play and sing LOW and HIGH while you play piano.

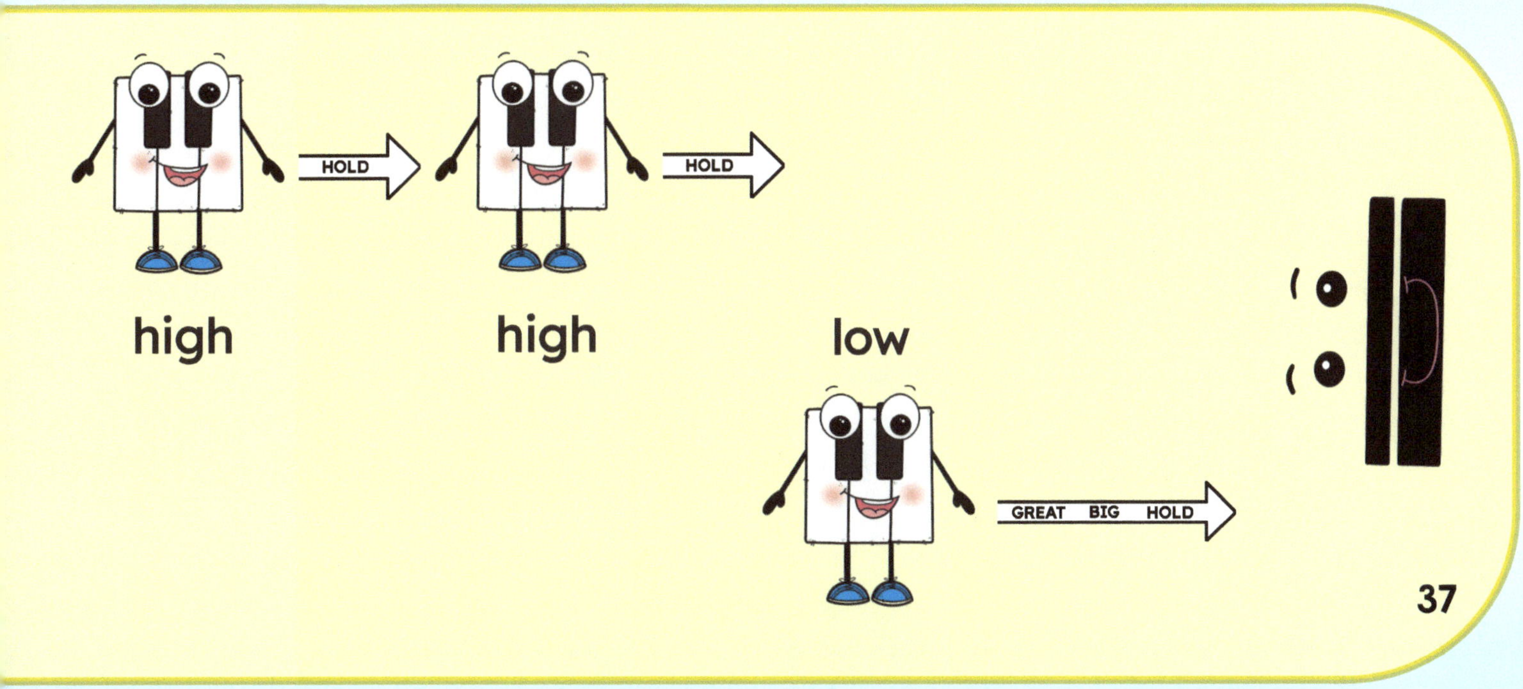

high → HOLD → high → HOLD → low → GREAT BIG HOLD →

Color a star each time you practice this song.

Tips for Practicing
Count slowly to three before you begin.
Tap the notes on your lap and sing LEFT and RIGHT.
Play and sing LEFT and RIGHT while you play piano.

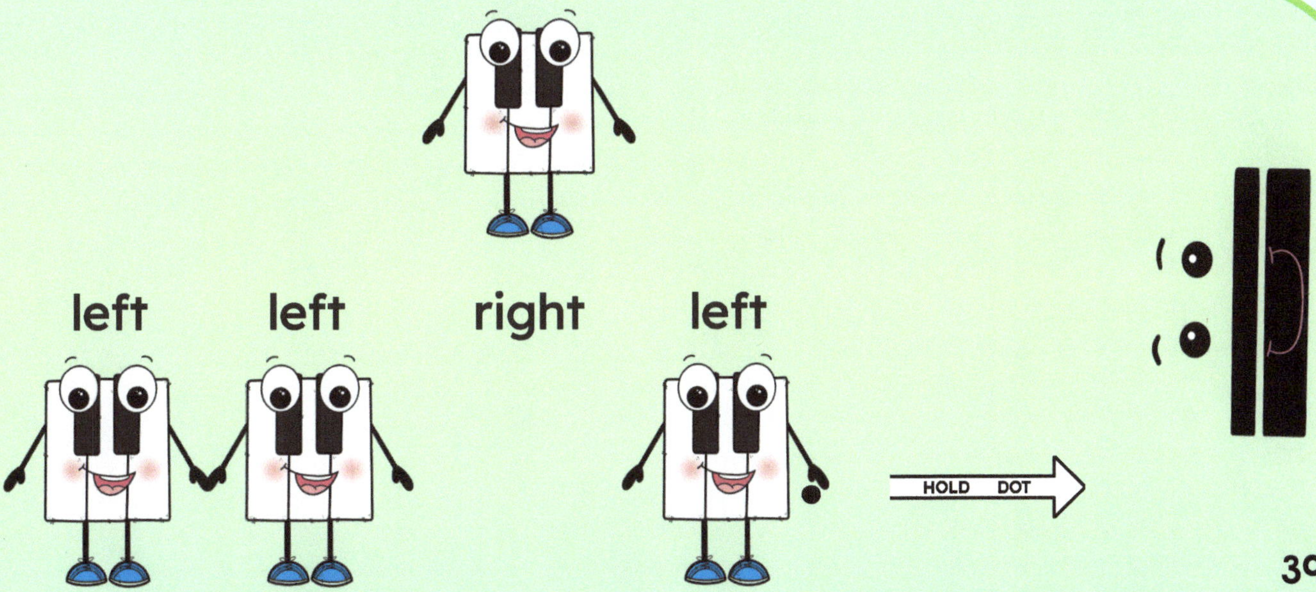

left left right left HOLD DOT

Let's Play Groups of 3!

Play **Threezie**'s black notes with Fingers 2, 3, and 4.
Can you find Missy Mouse, Parker Penguin, and Rosie Rabbit on your hand?

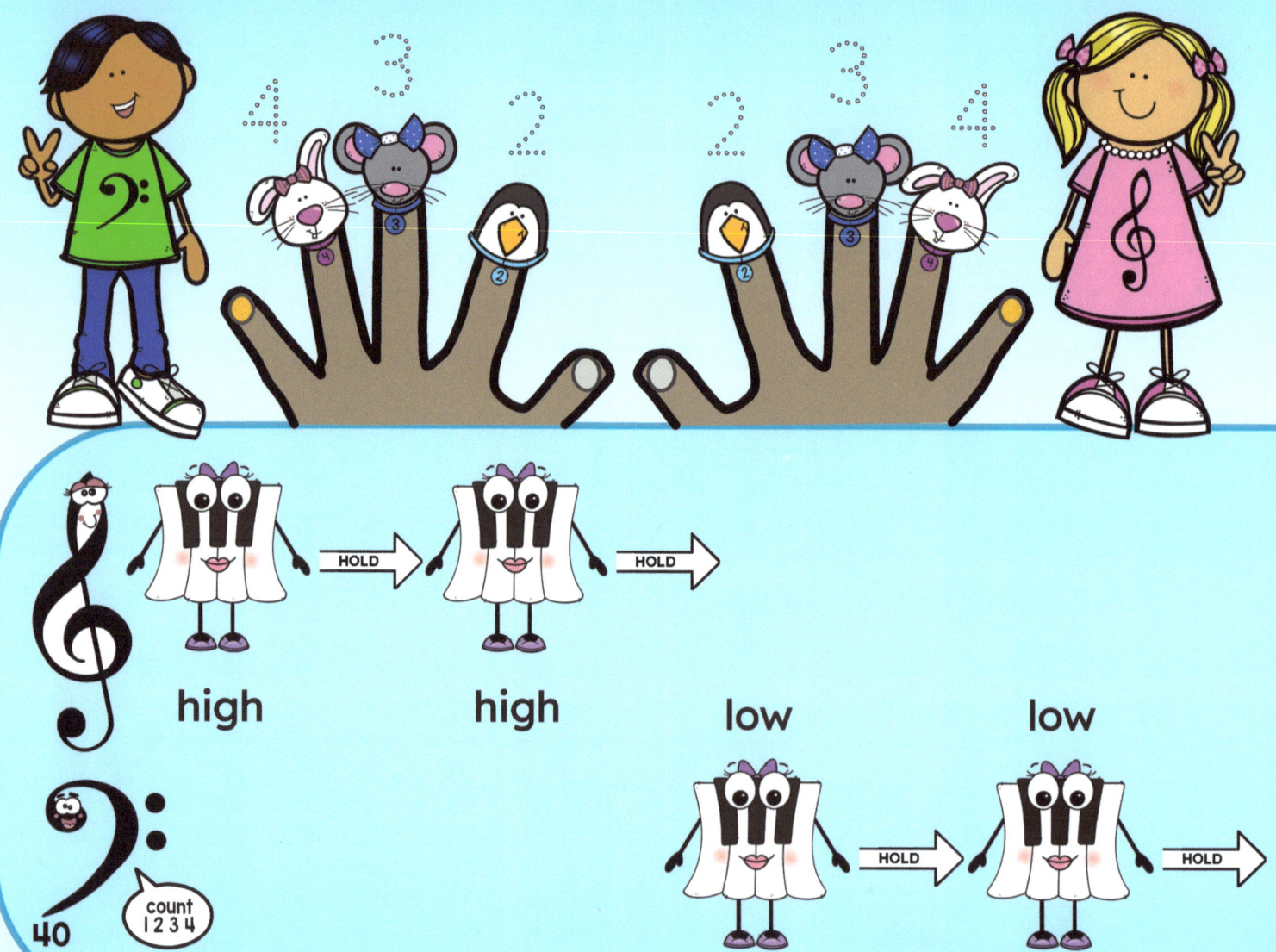

Color a star each time you practice this song.

Tips for Practicing

Count slowly to four before you begin.

Tap the notes on your lap and sing LOW and HIGH.

Play and sing LOW and HIGH while you play piano.

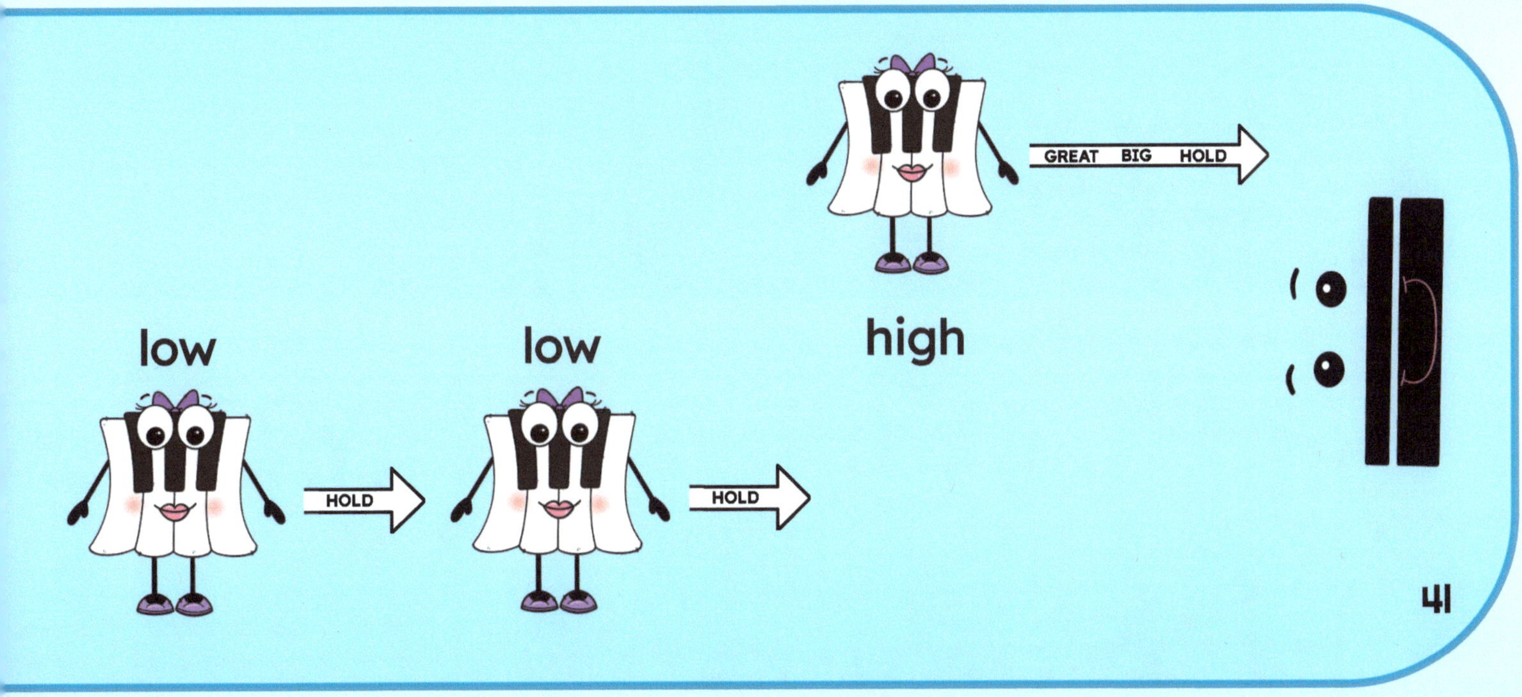

low → HOLD → low → HOLD → high → GREAT BIG HOLD →

I Love Low and High

Play **Threezie**'s black notes with Fingers 2, 3, and 4.
Can you find Missy Mouse, Parker Penguin, and Rosey Rabbit on your hand?

Color a star each time you practice this song.

Tips for Practicing
Count slowly to four before you begin.
Tap the notes on your lap and sing LOW and HIGH.
Play and sing HIGH and LOW, then try singing the words of the song.

I   love   low   and   high

GREAT BIG HOLD →

Tina's Rainbow

Play **Twoozie**'s black notes with Fingers 2 and 3.
Play **Threezie**'s black notes with Fingers 2, 3, and 4.

Color a star each time you practice this song.

Tips for Practicing
Count slowly to four before you begin.
Play and sing the words of the song.

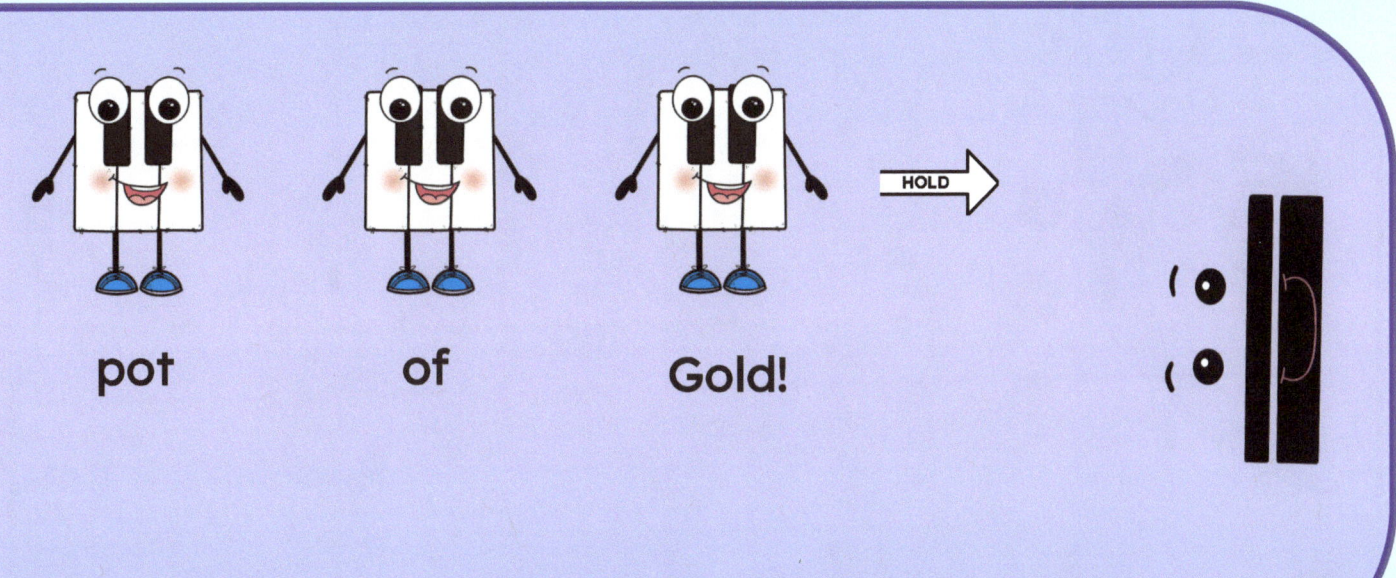

pot   of   Gold!

Bobby Bounces on Lilly Pads

Play **Twoozie**'s black notes with Fingers 2 and 3.
Play **Threezie**'s black notes with Fingers 2, 3, and 4.

Color a star each time you practice this song.

Tips for Practicing
Count slowly to four before you begin.
Play and sing the words of the song.

down   I   Go!

The Happy Dance

Play **Twoozie**'s black notes with Fingers 2 and 3.
Play **Threezie**'s black notes with Fingers 2, 3, and 4.

Dance   with   me,   ready   set   go,

Color a star each time you practice this song.

Tips for Practicing
Count slowly to three before you begin.
Play and sing the words of the song.

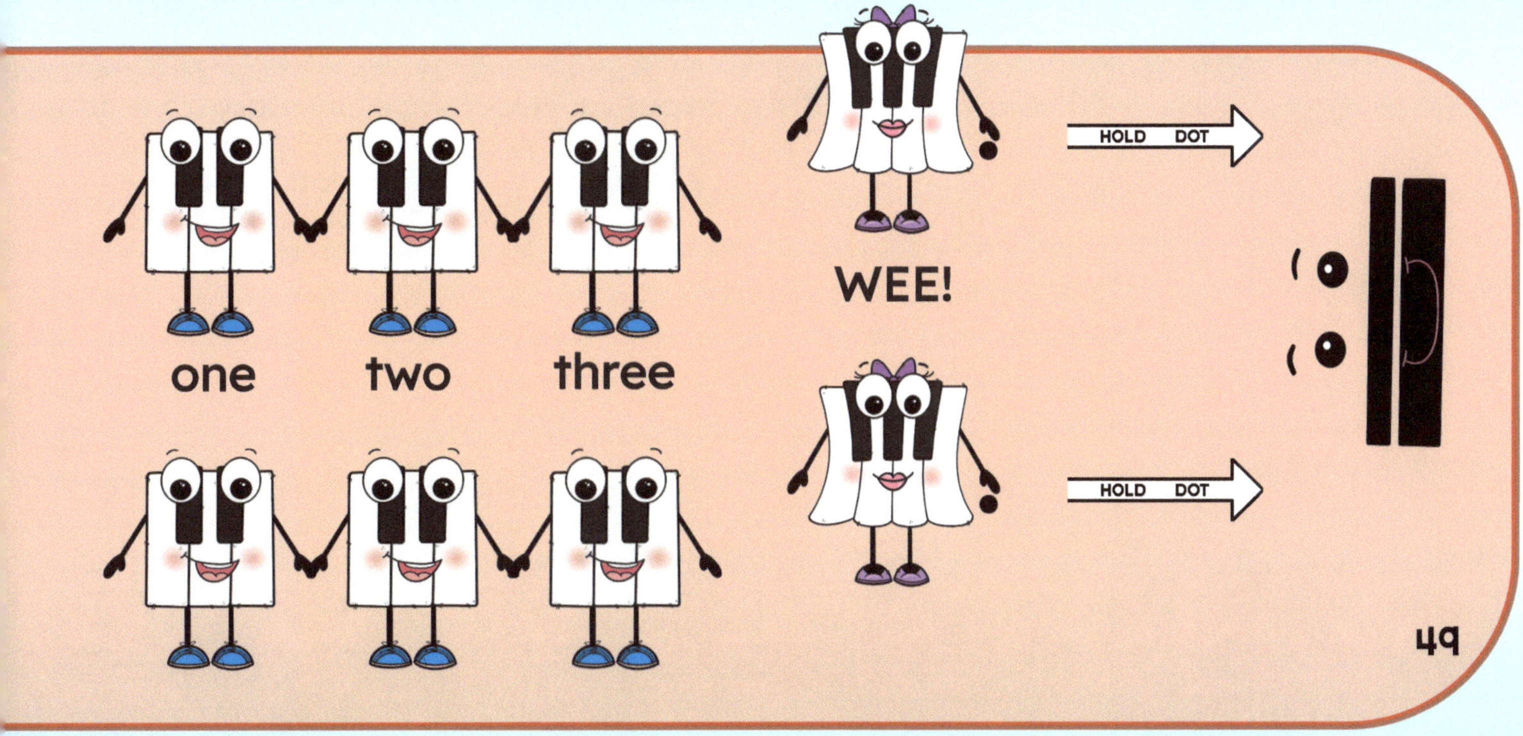

one   two   three   WEE!

HOLD DOT

HOLD DOT

ABOUT THE CREATORS

Debra Krol is a BC Registered Music Teacher who specializes in teaching music to babies, toddlers and preschoolers. She is also a children's songwriter and author. Ms. Deb enjoys camping with her hubby, kids, and Daisy Dog, their black and tan coonhound. She loves playing piano, ukulele, guitar and most of all, singing & drawing with all of her little friends!

 Tiny Tinkles Music Studio    tinytinkles

Corinne Orazietti was a preschool and elementary teacher for many years. She saw how her whimsical illustrations added sparkle to her lessons and decided it was time to share her passion for art with others. She now works as a full-time artist at her company, Chirp Graphics, and spends her days drawing cartoon dragons and fairies.

 chirpgraphics   chirpgraphicsclipart

Melanie Hawkins is an author, illustrator, elementary art teacher and mom to seven children! Her family is her greatest source of joy and inspiration. She enjoys camping, swimming, dark chocolate, and movie nights with her family. Melanie is an eternal optimist and wishes that everyone could see the world as she does with all of its beauty, hope and goodness.

 melaniehawkinsauthor.com   inspirejoypublishing

We are GROWING! More books in the series available soon!

   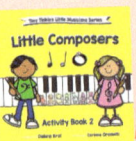    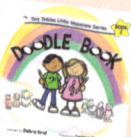  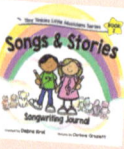

CONGRATULATIONS!

_____
Student's Name

has completed Little Performers Level 1 in the Tiny Tinkles Little Musician Series.

LEVEL 1

_____
Teacher

_____
Date